Kez Wickham St George

Essence

of

Life

Kez Wickham St George

Copyright 2025 by Kez Wickham St George

First published 2022

All rights reserved. No part of this book or its cover may be used or reproduced by any means, graphic, electronic, or mechanical, including photocopying, recording, taping or by any information storage retrieval system without the written permission of the copyright owner, except in the case of brief quotations embodied in critical articles and reviews.

Kez Wickham St George / Kez Publishing
Western Australia, Australia
kezwickhamstgeorge.com
ISBNS 978-1-7638692-4-0

Book Layout © womensbizglobal.com
Proofread by © Demelza St George
Book Cover ©Adam Bell photography
Cover design Andy Burns©andyscott.com.au

Essence of Life / Kez Wickham St George
2nd edition

DEDICATION

To the Power of Storytelling
Old habits do open new doors.
Be brave and step forward.

Index

DEDICATION	3
PROLOGUE	8
COLOURS OF ME	9
Quote #1	11
CAST OFF	12
Quote #2	14
WONKY WIRING	15
Quote #3	16
THE GALAHS	17
Quote #4	18
DRAWING THE LINE	19
Quote #5	21
SEA DANCER	22
Quote #6	23
WEDDING BELLS	24
Quote #7	25
Quote #8	28
EARTH, WIND & FIRE	29
Quote #9	31
FAITH	32
Quote #10	34
GIRLFRIENDS	35
Quote #11	37
THE LILLY	38

Quote #12	39
LAST KISS	40
Quote #13	42
MEMORIES	43
Quote #14	44
SMILE	45
Quote #15	46
MY GIRL	47
Quote #16	49
PAINTBALL	50
Quote #17	51
MY HAT	52
Quote #18	53
ANGEL IN MY ROOM	54
Quote #19	55
WISDOM	56
Quote #20	58
CAMPING	59
Quote #21	61
MY CASE OF MEMORIES	62
Quote #22	64
A SCAREDY BEER TALE	65
Quote #23	67
HE LOVES ME.	68
HE LOVES ME NOT.	68
Quote #24	70

PHONES	71
Quote #25	72
MY CALL	73
Quote #26	74
TO BE OR NOT TO BE	75
Quote #27	76
NIGHT TIDE	77
Quote #28	78
TIME	79
Quote #29	80
FRIENDSHIP	81
Quote #30	82
THOUGHTS	83
Quote #31	84
INSIDE YOURSELF	85
Quote #32	86
RETURN	87
TIMELESS	89
Quote #33	90
WHEN	91
Quote #34	93
MY KIGHT	94
Quote #35	95
COUNTRY GIRL	96
Quote #36	97
MY ARMCHAIR	98

Quote #37	99
WHAT IF	100
Quote #38	101
SUNFLOWER	102
Quote #39	103
TOGETHER	104
Quote #40	105
PEARL	106
Quote #41	107
STAND TALL	108
Quote #42	109
ENERGY	110
Quote #43	111
XMAS WISH	112
Quote #44	113
Quote #45	114
SILVER FISH	115
Quote #46	116
TIME OUT	117
Haiku	117
Quote #47	118
About The Author	119
Book Awards and Reviews	123
Testimonials of Mentorship	135

PROLOGUE

Was it something in the air I breathed, or was it in the exotic food I ate? Or in the wine? Perhaps it was something I sensed. No matter the how or why, this book was born while travelling through Europe. I remember very clearly not wanting to leave the magic of Ireland, a land I was connected to by family, or the charm and excitement of Spain. The Pyrenees inviting me to travel further afield, to walk through as many villages, towns, and cities as possible.

Alas, duty called me home to Australia. With my tattered, trusty notebook filled with poetry and quotes, I boarded the plane to Singapore. I had visited and toured Singapore before. However, this time, I wandered the streets of the city, not only tasting the local food but enjoying the poetic repartee of the vendors themselves. The essence of these countries now sat comfortably in my heart; this book is for the people who will never know the influence they had in the writing of Essence.

Kez

COLOURS OF ME

My heart was heavy,
its strings sang with grief.
Family and friends now parted,
my questions of how and why
not so brief.

New friends dried my tears,
words of wisdom uttered:
Relax and look inside of you
the answer is there to see.

I saw my spirit dance with joy,
one of love and grace.
I watched amazed
at its flight and pace.

My true colours I now know,
this is not denied:
Oceans of indigo,
forests of green,
blue skies that fill the eye.

A deep understanding flows in my blood,
not the questions
of where or why.

Kez Wickham St George

I emerged from a woman
who lay cocooned,
curled, awakening to my life of beauty.

Life is what I make of it,
not the emotional surging of others.

For I am a woman
of many strong passions,
now not caring if others don't see.

For it's my spirit
that now knows the difference
to be true
to the Colours of Me.

Essence of Life

Quote #1

*Believe in the magic of your dreams.
Live each day to the fullest.
As the future is your treasure.*

Kez Wickham St George

CAST OFF

Cast Off they cried,
tears of fear running freely down our faces.

Our hearts hammer like metal drums,
our joints of steel rusting in this
atmosphere.

We came to rescue
but we are the hunted.

Farewell, God speed
called our lone friend *Sea Dancer*.

Shadows of pelicans
on the white canvas point the way.
Tiny bubbles turn into star-studded foam
as we head off.

Red flying fish cry greetings
as they fly over our bow.

A raindrop captures
the explosion of our planet beneath us;
it morphs into the colour of rainbow
on spilled oil.

Essence of Life

Algae bloom still clings to the hull
as we lift
to wherever the wind blows us.

The faint twitter of land-locked birds fade
as we leave this angry planet
we once called our home.

Quote #2

While we worry about our life and happiness, life and happiness are unfolding around us.

WONKY WIRING

My wiring is wonky,
I yelled to blue sky.
My on light flickers sadly,
my stop light now fried.

My laugh button is sticky,
the tear bucket is full.
Eye buttons a tad worn out,
knee knobs don't pull.

My wires get sticky,
the battery is low.
My guzzle box clicky,
brain box goes slow.

My wiring's shonky,
my body breaking nonstop.
Where do I go to get fixed?
Why, the wonky wire shop.

Kez Wickham St George

Quote #3

Being concerned about what you don't have means ignoring what you do have.

THE GALAHS

They fly cloud-thick
with raucous cry,
wrenching dreams
from sleepy eye.

Pink breasts glowing
in the rising dawn,
they settle on treetops,
they cover dried lawn.

Pecking at grubs
deep in sandy holes,
nibbling berries
jealous chaos unfolds.

Waddling proudly,
nipping & screeching,
strutting their stuff.
All tells a story,
most of it bluff.

Then lifting as one
back into the sky,
swirling like storm clouds,
their calls echo
into a faint sigh.

Kez Wickham St George

Quote #4

*There are no coincidences in this life,
but recognising possibilities for new directions
and then boldly grabbing onto them.*

DRAWING THE LINE

In the realm of water
he was missed far and wide
the Silver Grandad of all Silver Fish,
once puffed with pride.

The large, scaled body
that would glide with ease,
or hurtle with hunger
at the smaller species.

They hid in nooks
and cranny aplenty,
shivering in fear
of Silver's tum always empty.

His mouth so wide
would snap with glee,
munching on shrimp
or sand-deep pipis.

Silver once famous
for craft and speed,
cheating death many times
he twisted and turned,
thrashing himself free
of line and man's greed.

Kez Wickham St George

Spitting disdain
at bent hook one last time,
soon his turn had come
of drawing the line.

Essence of Life

Quote #5

*Obstacles are simply
things that scare you
when you lose focus
on your goals.*

Kez Wickham St George

SEA DANCER

My eyes saw what the mind not believed:
a fair Damsel's form rose from the sea.

> Its hand waved in time
> with the waves flicking by,
> the sea now dark
> in tune with night sky.
>
> The red setting sun
> cast its shadow on wet sand.
> I stood in wonder
> to wave back or just stand?
>
> Was I the only one
> who saw this sea dancer,
> who danced on dark water,
> the moon and I her only grandstand?
>
> Was I the only one
> without any answers?
> Slowly, so gently,
> this maiden disappeared.
>
> Was I the only one
> who shed a sad tear?

Essence of Life

Quote #6

*A strong friendship will never die
if it's from the heart's core.*

Kez Wickham St George

WEDDING BELLS

Wedding bells ringing,
voices raised & singing.
Married bliss to be tested,
single thoughts now arrested.

"Congrats!" "Good on ya, mate!"
Bellowed forth through frothy brew.
Backslappers, hand shakers,
line up in a queue.

Rib nudges, eye winkers,
tired old jokes.
The bride rolls eye to sky
rude rugby club blokes.

Deep sigh escapes
from bridely bra.
'Tis cue for groom
to leave hot smoky bar.

Honeymoon beckons,
a trip so divine.
This time tomorrow
the Swiss Alpine.

Essence of Life

Quote #7

*Strength is what we gain
from the need to survive.*

Kez Wickham St George

DIVIDED IN TWO

Born into a land of mountains and water,
soil of black crumbling loam.
Snow-capped peaks piercing cotton ball clouds,
forest of thick lush green beauty
this is my heart's home.

A land of mist, damp muted bounty,
roaring thundering waterfalls.
Hot bubbling pools and steaming streams,
boutiques of dainty lacey ferns,
enclosed umbrella of vivid greens.

The country I live in
stretches mind, furrows brow
this huge land of abundance,
a time warp of past and now.

Your breath is stopped
as vastness is viewed,
eye not believing
what mind has imbued.

Ghost gums bleached white,
pale green dotted over rocks of burnt red.
Burnt tree trunks now spotted with bright

Essence of Life

green,
promise of life so deep
the eye cannot see.

Heat radiates from crevasse and pore,
pools of turquoise shiver with promise.
Yellow sand, red earth beg for more.

Bruised coloured sunsets bring deep shadows,
night's vast oval abounds.
Huge heavens filled with bright stars
sunrise to sunset
earthly beauty surrounds.

Kez Wickham St George

Quote #8

*Happiness can rely
on the quality of your thoughts.*

EARTH, WIND & FIRE

Fire erupts,
spitting out its red tongue with cackling glee.
Red in its rage, indigo and orange
within its mighty strength.

Black earth full of bounty,
virginal mounds of black loam await
to be filled with seed and pods
from ruined forests.

Winds blow the breath
of passion & strength
a race between green treasure
or searching beak.

Water gurgles gleefully
from rivulets and waterfalls,
falling in a rapture of melody,
a sensuous song.

Life once well-hidden
begins its journey,
to raise its face to bright sun,
earth admiring the beating of new life.

Her work for now is done.

Kez Wickham St George

All elements of life
is a mystery.

Essence of Life

Quote #9

*Be careful about what and who you tolerate
You may be teaching others
how to see you.*

Kez Wickham St George

FAITH

Whoever would have thought
one day I would be an elder
my advice trusted, heart-centred,
not always tactful or tender.

Whoever would have thought
what this life has taught me:
love can be spliced with logic,
no need for the emotional baggage in tow.
We, the elders, have struggled with this
and know.

How do you tell another,
one who thinks they know best,
the road you travelled was like no others
that was my life;
her life is yet to test.

Her journey is her very own,
made of laughter, love and life
with many blunders.

Her heart seems like it could break in two.
My advice is shrugged away,
her face scowling like black thunder.

Essence of Life

You want to hold her oh so close,
aching to follow ancient tradition.
Her angry tears hurting your heart,
your words of wisdom she tears apart.

Will your words leave an imprint
or a shadow
that hopefully one day
she too will follow her premonition.

Like no other:
the power of her own recognition.

Kez Wickham St George

Quote #10

Today and in all your tomorrows,
you will not be the same person
you were yesterday.

GIRLFRIENDS

Clatter, natter, china clinking,
candles inside glass hoods winking.
Dinner with friends
a bounty of chatter.

Have you heard?
Did you see?
No! she didn't…
questions buzz
like busy bees.

Bodies talk, jewelled hands a flutter
butterflies would envy
this female cluster.

Minds all saying
and thinking alike,
quick-witted laughter
rattles around,
many faces smiling,
so happy and bright.

News of born babies,
the male partner cast aside.
No tears does she shed,
this aging bride.

Kez Wickham St George

Age and body shapes
laughed at with glee
what's to discuss?
Ooh no, it's me.

They rustle and rummage
into bags of all shapes and sizes,
coloured memories paraded
like sought-after prizes.

With tears and wobbly grins,
we hug our farewells so tight,
promises made of meeting,
a future delight.

The power of my friends
so mighty and right.

Essence of Life

Quote #11

*When you pursue a life of contribution,
it also brings personal success.*

Kez Wickham St George

THE LILLY

Its roots bound deep
within unforgiving mud.

Tiny green shoots of life
creep into daylight.

One lone cone
of pale velvet waits.

A small white petal unfolds
in its centre,
a golden ray of hope.

Haiku
By Kez Wickham St George

Essence of Life

Quote #12

*Real opportunity for any success
lies within the person,
not the job.*

Kez Wickham St George

LAST KISS

Tell me you love me,
just say it the once.

Let my spirit
to what I pray
will be just.

Say you love me,
look into my eyes.
I want to believe you
harsh words
will carry no grace.

Please, say you love me,
for I know not what to do.

My heart feels crippled
inside this boney cage.

I see in your eyes
an empty void,
my plea unheard
now lost.

I knew my plight
was now a ghost.

Essence of Life

In your eyes their lay the truth
a death now claimed
from hopes and dreams.

Tomorrow
would bear its fruit.

Quote #13

Some people will never change.
Be grateful.

MEMORIES

A rush of memory
in one small stone.

His words of love
now encased
in a hard portal.

His small hand in mine
as he bequeathed to me
a promise of undying love,
his child's voice
strong and true.

Today he's moved
from my side.

The stone reminds me
every day

our heart beats
still strong with love.
I still feel
his hand in mine.

Kez Wickham St George

Quote #14

To shift your mindset
Change the way you think.

SMILE

A smile of welcome,
our open arms spread wide.

I step forward
to be embraced.

Apart for so long,
loneliness now ambushed
gone in a blink.

Together we stand,
united in our friendship.

Kez Wickham St George

Quote #15

Replace the thought: Why is this happening?
With: What is it trying to teach me?

MY GIRL

Her chuckle as a babe
made me smile.
It bubbled from deep
inside her belly,
then spilled into the room.

As a child,
her delight in everything new
would stop me
to ponder what she saw.
I too caught up in the magic
reflected in her eyes.

As a teen her smile faded,
anger flitting in her eyes
a warning of emotions.
Her laugh jaded
with complex devotions.
Who does she love
parents or lover more?

A woman now stands before me.
Her smile is faint,
the laughter not reclaimed.

Kez Wickham St George

For life has taught her many things:
    to trust another
    may hurt you
    in ways yet unknown.

Essence of Life

Quote #16

*There is always, always,
always something to be grateful for.*

Kez Wickham St George

PAINTBALL

My paintbox of colours,
many hues in a row.
My brush leaves a trail,
droplets of rainbows.

My paintbox dazzles,
putting jewellery to shame.
With each tinted drop
I see mystic worlds take shape.

They shimmer and dance
as my brush gently strokes,
each bright colour calling
the very best from us both.

Essence of Life

Quote #17

Life's like riding a bike.
To stay balanced, keep moving but stay on
the bike.

Kez Wickham St George

MY HAT

If the hat I wear is strickening and
Thickening
does it make my mind scrunched up or
munched up?

If we swapped hats
how would I feel?
Would I be called a fish or an eel
would I be you or you be me?

To wear your hat would I still be me
or would my face change
a face you could not see?

In my hat your face would be wobbly
'cause my hats much more knobbly.
My hats been scuffed, my hats been bruised,
my hats are worn, your hat hardly used.

I like your hat it suits you good and bold,
I like my hat as time has told.

So let's not swap but just agree
I can't be you and you can't be me.

It's not your hat I choose to wear,
my heart not your hat that holds you dear.

Essence of Life

Quote #18

*It's not about the goal,
It's about growing
to become
that person
who can achieve that goal.*

Kez Wickham St George

ANGEL IN MY ROOM

A faded painting in my room
of an angel giving prayer.
No sees her but myself,
no one says a word.

At night, as I lay
with sleep-tired eyes,
the house creaking
its aged bones,

I nestle deep into my bed,
wind and rain
beating on windows.

There is no fear,
as I know she's there
a beacon of safety and love.
There is angel in my room.

Essence of Life

Quote #19

*Make a promise to yourself
To thrive and survive,
Celebrate each day.
In some way or another.*

Kez Wickham St George

WISDOM

In a buoyant sea where I lay,
a tiny seed of humanity
kicking and stretching
in this warm brine,
a learning of survival ahead of me.

Listening to her beating heart,
I know it's nearly time.
Quietly we have joined,
soon to be torn apart.
Learning so much
in this red twilight ocean,
knowledge so wise
that this choice was mine.

Now pushed into a world
of confusing emotions,
I soon learn to sit upon knee,
gaining my fill of old age wisdoms.
The words that are spoken,
filled with a musical potion.

I learnt on this knee
that words can harm
words can stroke you with love
or sadden the heart.

Essence of Life

Her whispered wisdom
leaked deep into my soul.
I'm grateful for her love of words
her wisdom was my gain.

Kez Wickham St George

Quote #20

*No matter the size or shape,
ethnicity or religion,
everyone can
change the course
of their future.*

Essence of Life

CAMPING

Faces smiling, greetings friendly,
away from your workday life
neither full nor empty.

Voices welcoming, saying hello,
their frantic lifestyle now on go slow.
Green domes rising, brown ones too,
little tin boxes on wheels passing through.

Tent ropes tight and twangy,
sounds of hammers thwacking pegs.
Webs of ropes arise
to catch one's legs.

People laughing, greeting old mates and new
Hi, how ya going? How's the world with you?
What did this year bring? Travels near and far,
a story is forthcoming, it's their turn to star.

I sit and listen, laugh and sigh
to the tale of a far-off land.
It's proving hard to stay awake
his story very grand.

The sun sinks low,
casting its grand glow.

Kez Wickham St George

All is quiet now as campers go to asleep.
I too join those in slumber deep.

Essence of Life

Quote #21

Be the reason someone feels welcome, valued, loved, and supported.

Kez Wickham St George

MY CASE OF MEMORIES

Memories, love won and lost,
of friends past and dear with melancholy,
faded photos precious with wear.

Tatty, torn finger paintings,
strange stick figures all in a line.
Mummy and Daddy in wriggly letters
to me they're all divine.

Trinkets of all sorts abound in this box:
shells, stones, feathers, handmade cards
recollections from many ports.

Memories so strong, an unbreakable bind.
My children's voice calling, *"Look what I've
found!"*
Their baby faces so proud
of this important find.

My family has grown - to some I'm not
known.
Memories of laughter as we all take our
place,
pulling funny faces,
the camera seals our fate.

Essence of Life

A life full of riches - I'm so glad it's mine.
A bounty of memories, some good, some bad,
tucked aside for another time.

Kez Wickham St George

Quote #22

*If I'm constantly scratching at misfortunes,
reacting instead of acting,
mourning the past
or praying for a better future
instead of living in today,
I am missing out on what the universe
is trying to show me.*

A SCAREDY BEER TALE

Once upon a time
there was a village Rhyme
that folk from near and far did chant
a song of cheer
about the virtues of wine and beer.

But some folks from here and there
whispered these two brews to fear,
and so forbid the naughty rhyme
while others brewed a stronger fear.

They brewed it in a cauldron huge
it had such a lovely smell.
Spice and yeast, a dash of green herbs,
claims a sniff or smell
would make you well.

Now folks heard this silly rhyme:
that beer is bad for you,
to be on guard was wise.
Large letters bold with two crossed bones
was stuck to either side.

Wonder brew now sold in every shop
this brew cleans out tubes and all.

Kez Wickham St George

*Drink this beer, it's good for you,
just chug until you pop!*
There is a lesson for all to tell:
this silly rhyme is not a spell.

There was a reason it was called
a brew from hell.

Quote #23

*Is home to your heart just a place to stay,
or is it a place where you are loved
and love in return?*

Kez Wickham St George

HE LOVES ME.
HE LOVES ME NOT.

He loves me, he loves me not,
ring a ring a rose's,
rock, paper, scissors - another game.
All can make you see,
but add no blame.

Tissue paper strength unknown
covers rock of grief and sorrow,
stopping streaming fall of tears,
damming hurt of endless fears.

Scissors wait, blades set to snap or slice,
cutting cords of beliefs - now no strings to
tie.
Heart do break, melt and crumble,
spirit drags with deadly weight.
Pray to rock for safety's sake.

As you hide inside this place of grace,
your faith in rock a safety place.
Scissors poke, snip and click,
sharp points will snap when rock shows its
power.
Paper is its shrouds to cover sparked
shower.

Essence of Life

Don't fret or fear - you're safe.
Within this rock you can hide.

Kez Wickham St George

Quote #24

*We are made for both joy and woe;
the more we accept this,
the better we navigate through life.*

PHONES

From wall to bench to pocket
it happened in a flash.
One day I was winding a handle,
all changed with speed,
it seemed so fast and brash.

Long ago a voice
would greet me kindly.
She would even know my name.
We would spend a while swapping stories,
then back to our chores once again.

Years went by
the telephone now small,
now sat on bench,
not attached to wall.

It had a dial that whirred once turned,
instant connection
with friends insured.

Today this phone, so small,
is placed in a pocket.
A number is tapped, no dial in sight
what next, we all wonder,
with our human delight.

Quote #25

*We all need a lighthouse in our lives
to warn us when danger is near
or to cast a comforting light
to help us find our way home.*

MY CALL

From a distance
you will hear my call,
the notes rising high,
buffeting edges
of scudding clouds.

Once released,
the cascade drops,
raining down
into the leafy canopies.

Who will listen
as they fall?

Kez Wickham St George

Quote #26

*There are no coincidences in this world;
only recognition of passing possibilities
taking a new direction
and then boldly grabbing hold of it.*

TO BE OR NOT TO BE

My name has been forgotten.
My body once repelled Neptune's waves
a craft so fine
oceans parted before me.

Sand now drifts
where sea once curled.
Joints rust
under flotsam of salted years.

My demise is near,
my heart is broken.
I silently weep
for the love shared between us.

My last heart spark
leaps with joy.

Today the sun
floods my wooden ribs.
I now hear
a whispered invitation

To be embraced
within salty depths.

Kez Wickham St George

Quote #27

*Anything the mind believes and conceives
It will achieve.*

NIGHT TIDE

Sliding, rolling, gliding
a wave of prism colours
meets the shore.

Its passionate boom
becomes a hissing sigh,
releasing the stories
of sailors long gone

its journey now done.

… Kez Wickham St George

Quote #28

It's in the moments of any decision
that your destiny is shaped.

TIME

There came a time
when my own light dimmed low,
my heartbeat in time
to a pulse slowed with fear.

There came a time
when mine eyes saw no beauty
trapped in a cage of jagged bones,
blood pulsed into deep pools.

There came a time
when a voice of light found me,
a whisper like a sea of rolling mist.
I clung to the bare ribs
of my own sinking ship.

There came a time
when my own voice became raised in salute
calling those still in dark places,
cowering in the shades
of their own earthy vessels.

Kez Wickham St George

Quote #29

If you think education is not important
Try living with ignorance.

FRIENDSHIP

I would hold you close once more
    to say those words
    I could not before.

I would hold you close,
look into your eyes,
explore the sadness,
break down those walls.

I would hold you close
to simply ask why —
your friendship to me well earnt,
not tied to some device.

For friends we are
in body and heart,
a jigsaw of colours,
dancing patterns of light.

I would hold you close
to delay
your earthly flight.

Kez Wickham St George

Quote #30

*Sift through the sands of offered advice,
finding your own pearl of wisdom.*

THOUGHTS

My thoughts drip down
over my hull of scuttled dreams.

Emotions roll
like storm-tossed waves
over razor-sharp reefs,

parted now
by my desire
for safe harbour

connected only
with Neptune's cord.

Quote #31

Remember, you are the creation
of ten thousand love stories.
Your name was uttered in the heavens
before you came into being.
Your purpose here is to
simply be who you are.

INSIDE YOURSELF

Dance to your own tune,
march to your own beat.

You have more inside you
than most.

People will begin to know
that now is the time to use
your own skills and knowledge,

to bring out
just who you are.

Create a new path
for you have greatness
within you.

Kez Wickham St George

Quote #32

*Never walk on a well-trodden path;
it only leads to where others have already been.*

RETURN

If I could return
to the places I once knew
and meet those folks
that I once called mine,

I would take that chance
and greet them,
just to sit with them and listen
once more
to the tales of what was.

I would tell them my story,
as now I can add
that my life was very different
sometimes happy,
sometimes sad.

If I could meet them
one more time,
to sit and listen
to their stories, not mine,

I would take great pleasure
in adding my story
my words cascading, then blending

Kez Wickham St George

into the lines
of our past history.
To lay my head down
in its need to rest,
to close my eyes,
no need to fear
for I'm now with those
that I held dear.

TIMELESS

Time is slow for those who wait.
Fast for those who lament.
Short for those that celebrate.
But for those of us who love
Time is eternity.

William Shakespeare

Quote #33

*Progress is a step in the right direction,
but it is not necessarily a step forward.*

WHEN

"When is it the right time?"
said the caterpillar to the sun.

"When the time is right,"
the sun warmly replied.

"Will the wind tell me?" she asked.
The sun beamed its mirth
as the caterpillar stretched and basked.

"When is the right time?"
she asked the wind.

The wind shook with glee, saying,
"it's written in your memory."

"Will the rain tell me?"
she wanted to know.
The rain answered back,
"Before the snow."

They were all correct,
as time would tell.
Her heart said, "It's time
to weave your cocoon spell."

Kez Wickham St George

The seasons changed
as she slept on,
safely curled
from the winter's storm.

The sun's bright rays
woke her winter slumber.
Wings of white emerged
from the pod
of silken wonder.

Quote #34

Follow your heart and your destiny,
for this is your life.
There is nowhere else to go,
is there?

Kez Wickham St George

MY KIGHT

For many years
I did wonder,
applauding your shining success,
cringing at my own blunders.

I had prayed for such a long time
for this knight in his armour
to whisk me away,
save me from my life's drama.

Then one day I realised
I had stepped from frypan to fire.
My knight not so bold,
his opinion always dire.

My life becoming stressful,
every step taken with care.
My knight now my jailer,
his words a constant fear.

His love for me no longer,
he had not been what he seemed.
I wonder where the magic went,
or if it was all a dream.

Quote #35

Love is the best medicine in life's score.
Without it, one would forever
be out of tune in the vast choir of humanity.

Kez Wickham St George

COUNTRY GIRL

Scuffed jean,
faded jeans,
ponytail hair.

Bronzed skin,
brown eyes,
freckles spread across cheeks.
Laughter readily spills,
generous smiles shared.

Quote #36

Empowerment

Empowerment is the sweet nectar from bushland that has blossomed after chaos has ravaged our earth.

Kez Wickham St George

MY ARMCHAIR

It sits like a waiting servant,
waiting for me, its owner,

to heave a heavy sigh
as my body lowers its limbs
into the cushiony depths.

Essence of Life

Quote #37

Why repeat the same old mistakes
if there are many to learn from?

Kez Wickham St George

WHAT IF

What if our religion was each other?
If our practice was our life?
If prayer were our everyday words?
What if the temple was the Earth?

If the forests were our churches,
if holy water was the lakes, rivers and oceans
and what if meditation
was our relationship?

If the teacher was life?
If wisdom was self-knowledge?
And if Love
was the centre of our being?

Author unknown

Essence of Life

Quote #38

*Many of us overlook the small joys of life
while chasing our own happiness.*

Kez Wickham St George

SUNFLOWER

Wind gently nudges
tall, elegant stems.

Like bright lights,
their open faces sway
each seeking the light.

Quote #39

*There are people who speak to us
but do not listen.*

*There are people who will hurt us deeply
but leave no scar.*

*Then there are those people
who simply appear in our lives
And will leave a mark on it forever.*

Kez Wickham St George

TOGETHER

The power of these times
lies in the rise of our equal leadership

standing together to find
balance and solutions
to the earth's problems.

President J F Kennedy

Essence of Life

Quote #40

*Take what is good from your past
and build your future from it.*

Kez Wickham St George

PEARL

Wet, hard, barnacle-encrusted shell,
   clamped tightly over bounty,
   inherited fear from birth.

   Jaw of muscle clamped open,
   invasion of womb-like meat
   shuddering, aching surrender
   of bounty ocean-deep.

   Birth from virginal hiding,
   illustrious perfect orb residing.
   Mother of fortune cast aside,
   globe of fame and fortune rising.

Essence of Life

Quote #41

*What you face now
will help you get through it.*

Kez Wickham St George

STAND TALL

There were times
when I wanted to yell
from the highest of mountains
I have a voice,
listen to me.

There were times
when I wanted the rich & famous
to enfold me in their dreams,
to be one with them.

Now, as I look back,
power of the ancients
sings through my veins.
No longer do I seek approval.

Essence of Life

Quote #42

*A person without a goal
is like a ship without a rudder.*

Thomas Carlyle

ENERGY

If you intend your life with passion,
create a vision not a mission.
Why weary the body with toil,
when the mind will till the fertile soil.

Breathe in the air
of mountain or ocean,
blood flowing freely
to energize motion.

Feel the deep thud
of a grateful heart,
embrace your life force
from the very start.

Essence of Life

Quote #43

*We are all self-made
but only the successful
will admit it.*

Earl Nightingale

Kez Wickham St George

XMAS WISH

How I loved to hold
their small hands in mine,
to stare at the night sky.

With each scudding cloud
we would see
Santa's sleigh

As years went by,
growth from child to adult,
we still gathered on Xmas Eve
tradition in its place.

My heart ached to hear
the magic of childish awe,
when a hand slipped into mine,
a whispered voice claiming:
I see reindeer
dancing in a line.

Essence of Life

Quote #44

*We can think those were the days
or believe I'm living my dream.*

Kez Wickham St George

Quote #45

*Don't compromise yourself.
You're all you've got.*

SILVER FISH

In a clear pond of aqua blue,
made by the distant ocean,
the tide had swept clean
the shoreline dotted with seabirds.

Each black beady eye
waiting for me to leave,
their silver prey
swimming
innocently.

I was their guardian,
a duty I had not asked for.
I hunch over them, knowing
certain death was blowing
in the Indian Ocean wind.

Quote #46

*Even the best of us
sometimes
have to eat our own words.*

Essence of Life

TIME OUT

Time is all we have.
We are clocked in from birth.
The clock stops, as does destiny.

Haiku
By Kez Wickham St George

Kez Wickham St George

Quote #47

*Each of us
creates our universe around us
when we should be creating
it within us.*

About The Author

'We are all Unique Walking Stories Just Waiting to be Told.'
Kez Wickham St George is a 5-Star Gold Award-Winning Best-Selling Author whose influence in the literary world is profound and far-reaching. Acclaimed as a highly gifted speaker, global writer's consultant, and leader in her profession, Kez's wisdom and passion have touched countless lives. Her dedication to championing people from diverse backgrounds to tell their stories and write with passion is at the core of her work.
With multiple best-selling books and two prestigious Gold Titan Awards to her name, Kez is recognised as a literary force to be reckoned with. Her storytelling prowess and commitment to creative writing have earned her numerous literacy awards and accolades, including the People's Choice Able Book Awards. A true global citizen, Kez has

spoken nationally and internationally, sharing her knowledge about the process of writing, editing, and producing all forms of written communication. She is widely travelled, and her experiences have shaped her expansive authorship, encouraging others to think outside the box and redefine what authors can achieve in the digital age.

Kez's work has been celebrated by two royal families in the UK and Sweden, and she either coordinated and coauthored over twelve anthologies, including one on the lives of eighteen international women and another with Michiko Sato, featuring authors and artists from Ako, Japan. With fourteen books to her name, including a celebrated trilogy, a collection of poems and quotes, and a recent anthology with #mmhpress, this book is her first book of Fables.

Kez continues to captivate readers with her diverse and compelling narratives. In her Western Australian community, Kez is known for her efforts to empower others to write, creating writers' workshops and giving back through her volunteer work with Global Book Reviews. She has co-produced and co-hosted a weekly international show that highlights the work of authors and artists from around the world. Her creative energies and refreshing idealism are reflected in her consistent dedication to her craft, culminating in a short film adaptation of the prologue from her novel Scribe, which was shown in theatres across Australia.

Beyond her literary achievements, Kez is a prominent figure in the media, contributing to numerous magazines and co-hosting TV and radio shows where she shares her passion for personal development and women's global access to resources. Kez believes in the power of education for all women globally, seeing it as the key to achieving equality. She encourages everyone to express themselves through art, no matter the genre, and her favourite quote, *'we are all unique walking stories just waiting to be told'* embodies her approach to life and work.

Ready to elevate your writing career?
Contact Kez for expert mentoring, book promotion, or to gain visibility through her renowned book reviews. With her extensive experience and passion for storytelling, Kez is here to help you gain the recognition you deserve.

www.kezwickhamstgeorge.com

Book Awards and Reviews

The Story Tellers Series
Jigsaw
Book 1 in the Storytellers Series 2023
Literary Titan Review ⭐⭐⭐⭐⭐

Kez Wickham St George is an engrossing and emotionally charged narrative that delves into the Deeply concealed world of Parental childhood Trauma. At the heart of this tale is Cassie, the protagonist who endures a life riddled with abuse and neglect within the confines of her family home, desperately yearning. For love and acceptance. Compelled into a marriage with a narcissistic alcoholic as a result of her families Cult like obligations. Cassie is faced with the bleak choice of either succumbing to despair or embarking. On a courage journey to discover her true self. Throughout the narrative the author skilfully Weaves themes of escape, love, resilience, and the Patriarchal systems cruel oppression while exploring the enigmatic paranormal aspects that entwine themselves in Cassie's life. Jigsaw is a poignant, gripping Masterpiece, adeptly unwavering the profound story of a child growing through the profound abuse into the success story we have before us today.

Tapestry
Book 2 in the Storytellers Series 2024
Literary Titan Review ☆☆☆☆

Tapestry is an intricate, multi-generational tale that weaves together the stories of women who have been marginalised and oppressed but are fiercely resilient. Set against the backdrop of historical periods where patriarchy, sexism, and injustice reigned supreme, the book tells the stories of women like Aida and Rosalie, whose lives were marked by pain but also by fortitude and wisdom. At its core, the book is a tribute to the strength of ancestral female wisdom and the persistence of the human spirit. What struck me immediately was the rawness of the storytelling. There's something visceral in how the author portrays Aida's life in the 1700s. The imagery of her as a child left to survive in a pigpen, later abused, and sold, but ultimately rising to become a healer, was both heartbreaking and triumphant. The writing captures not just the brutality of her circumstances, but also her inner strength and resilience, particularly when she delivers babies and saves lives with her herbal knowledge.

While the stories are compelling, the pacing in some sections, like Petra's story in the convent, was slower and more introspective, while other parts, such as the vivid descriptions of Rosalie's journey on the convict ship, were packed with action and emotion. The lengthy descriptions and heavy use of historical context sometimes pulled me out of the emotional depth of the characters' journeys. I would've loved more balance between the historical backdrop and the intimate personal moments that define these women's lives.

Another standout element is how the book dives into themes of female solidarity. The interactions between Aida, Ursula, and the group of women they eventually join in the woods felt empowering. Despite being rejected by society, these women form their own community, sharing knowledge and supporting one another. That part of the book, to me, was a beautiful ode to the strength of women when they come together. The detailed descriptions of the forest life, food gathered, and herbal remedies they concocted made these scenes feel rich and alive.

Tapestry is a bold and sweeping story that showcases the harsh realities faced by women throughout history but also their incredible resilience and ability to thrive despite it all. I would recommend this book to readers who enjoy historical fiction with deep emotional depth and a strong focus on female empowerment.

Review by Annie Gibbins Women's Biz Global

"A Masterpiece of Resilience and Ancestral Legacy"

Kez Wickham St George has crafted a remarkable and evocative novel in Tapestry: The Book of Lost Worlds. This book is a profound exploration of the courageous women who defied societal norms, battled against the injustices of their times, and left an indelible mark on history. Wickham St George's storytelling prowess shines as she weaves together the lives of these women, creating a rich tapestry of narratives that are both heart-wrenching and inspiring.

Through the lens of these brave female ancestors, the novel delves into themes of resilience, strength, and the enduring impact of ancestral legacies. The author masterfully captures the emotional depth and complexities of each character, allowing readers to connect with their struggles and triumphs on a deep personal level. The vivid descriptions and historical contexts enrich the narrative, bringing to life the harsh realities faced by women who fought against the constraints of religion, sexism, and societal expectations.

The prose is lyrical and haunting, with each chapter serving as a testament to the fortitude of these women. Wickham St George's ability to intertwine these stories with a sense of reverence for the past makes Tapestry a compelling and unforgettable read. This book not only honours the memory of those who came before but also serves as a powerful reminder of the strength and resilience that lies within all of us.

Tapestry: The Book of Lost Worlds is more than just a historical novel; it is a celebration of the human spirit and the enduring power of storytelling. It is a must-read for anyone who appreciates rich, character-driven narratives that explore the complexities of history and the legacy of those who dared to stand against the tide. Kez Wickham St George has created a literary gem that will resonate with readers long after the final page is turned.

Review by Geoff Bailey USA book reviews

Tapestry book 2 of the Storyteller Trilogy by Kez St. George is a beautifully told series of stories from her family ancestral record. Each chapter and character captured beautifully with a caring authority that has shown compassion for the hard life of her ancestors. Being a huge genealogy fan and consider collections like Tapestry to be so important for us to understand who we are and where we come from. Reading Tapestry made me appreciate New Zealand where the Author originated from and now resides in Australia. I consider stories and memoirs like those in Tapestry such an important capture of a people, their cultures their lives, and their histories. I would go as far to say I found Tapestry a true national treasure, and no doubt a bestseller. Thank you for an entertaining and enlightening read Kez Wickham St. George.

The People's Choice Award
Able Book Awards
2024

The Campfire Trilogy
Metal Mermaid - *Book 1 of the series*
No #1 Amazon Best Seller in 5 categories and 6 countries
Titan Gold & Silver awards medallions
mmhpress Gold award
WA Literati recommendations award.

Essence of Life

Literary Titan Review ⭐⭐⭐⭐⭐

Metal Mermaid 5-star Review by Titan by Kez Wickham St George is a beautifully written memoir that takes readers on a spiritual and physical adventure. Tara and her husband Russ set off on a journey to explore Western Australia, but unexpected events quickly change their plans. Tara's journey of self-discovery takes her on a new path, one that challenges her both physically and emotionally. She meets fellow travellers and experiences the joys of the caravanning world, making her way from Australia's upper coast to New Zealand's northern island.

In this thought-provoking book, Wickham St George skilfully weaves a tale of courage, resilience, and determination that is both inspiring and captivating. The author's descriptive writing style transports readers to the various locations Tara visits, allowing them to feel the change of seasons and experience the heat and cold of the land. The side characters in the book are equally intriguing, with rich backstories and tales of their own. Metal Mermaid is an immersive memoir that provides readers with clear insight into the caravanning world and introduces them to various cultures.

Wickham St George's straightforward writing style makes the book an easy and engaging read. The book is infused with culture and worldly sights, and readers will feel like they are part of Tara's journey. Metal Mermaid is an outstanding book that I highly recommend to readers looking for inspirational that showcases the beauty of life's Journey. The authors ability to tell such a captivating story that takes its readers on a spiritual journey is nothing short of Impressive. Metal Mermaid is an outstanding book that I highly recommend to readers looking for an inspirational book that highlights the beauty of life's journey. The author's ability to tell a captivating story that takes readers on a spiritual adventure is nothing short of an impressive literature experience.

The Cuppa Tree - Book 2 of the series

A story of a woman who lived loved and learned caravaning in the outback. Sit around the metaphorical campfire with author Kez Wickham St George as she brings you on an unexpected journey throughout the pages of The Cuppa Tree. This natural-born storyteller will share tales from experiences and stories shared on her travels around Australia.

Scribe

Book 3 of the series
When Tara, the lead character, finds herself battling illness and snowstorms in the far South Island of New Zealand, she is called a catalyst for what she is being asked to do: die. "The world is in a state of great change," she is told. We, the greater good, ask you to Scribe for the deceased, those who have not told their stories before they passed over.

Co- authored Anthology's
Hear us Roar 2025 KMD publisher. A bestselling anthology that brings the hearts together, powerful short stories told by an array of global authors.

55 faces Inspire 2024
No #1 Amazon Best Seller. An anthology that embraces many women of many dialects and ethnicities. An inspirational book that will have you reaching out to be part of the next book due out in 2025

Rising into greatness by worthy women.com 2025.
No #1 Amazon Best Seller. A collection of heartwarming stories who will inspire you to live life on your terms.

Memoirs of Successful Women
Memoirs of Successful Women is a collection of stories from women who have lived, breathed, and elevated their brand.
Women's Biz Publishing. 2023

The Colors of Me
The Colors of Me is a multinational contribution of 18 authors, each one sharing her empowering and inspirational story.

Inspired Connections
Unleashing the Magic of Deeper Relationships
No #1 Amazon in 37 categories – 2021/2023

There will be many roadblocks and many dysfunctions along the way. Your job in life is to sort out the noise and nonsense, to trust your intuition and acknowledge your own truth.

Hille House Publishing. 2021

Build Your Success
Leadership Tips from the World's Best CEO's and Leaders

A co-authored book that sheds light on leadership and many success tips from the world's best leaders and Mentors. Critical thinkers and role models who have proven success, built on ideology plus uncovering the essential tools for risk-taking, goal setting, and most of all purpose.

Testimonials of Mentorship

From Sandy Skelton Publisher / Editor Ozark.

There is simply something magical about Kez. She is brilliant, honest, transparent, and forthright. From the moment we met, I knew I'd found a kindred spirit whose mission is to extend a hand to lift up others following in our footsteps or carving their own similar path. Kez reviewed my publishing house Ozark Press's first publication The Power to Rise Above. That experience ensured that she will be a part of my writer's journey forevermore. At whatever stage you are at in your writing journey, engaging Kez in your project will improve it immeasurably. You are in safe hands. With more sharks out there in the book coaching arena, it is refreshing to meet a genuine soul like Kez who wants your book to shine and openly shares her extensive knowledge and expertise

From Nicola Mary Burton. Author of 'The One.

To Kez Wickham St George Publisher. There's not enough space, to say what my heart feels for your dedication, your hours of work, creativity, teachings, guidance, wisdoms, inspirations, The beginning of first the few words that I gave you, that you magically transformed for this book. A profound mentor, coach, and structural editor. More importantly, your ability to see me, in my true colours and vulnerability. For being my safe harbor throughout the many storms, I traversed in the true spirit of writing. I thank you, with all my beingness, for who I have become, as a writer and published author. I will continue to aspire, to dig deep into my inner muse, as you are forever my Guiding Inspiration.

From Patti Stueland Author of 'Living Your Best Dash.'

A part of living your best Dash, are the people you choose to surround yourself with. God has blessed me with so many incredible people over my lifetime and continues to do so. One of those incredible blessings has been to meet and collaborate with my structural editor and co-publisher Kez Wickham St. George. I first met Kez as a guest on my podcast, "Rediscovering your Passion and Purpose with Patti." Listening to her talk about how enthusiastic she is about helping women to tell their stories really touched me deeply. When I knew it was time to get going on this project, Kez was the first person I thought of to share this DASH book idea. She loved it.

Through her guidance, encouragement, support, and knowledge, I have now recently completed my book Living Your Best Dash, where my mentor Kez Wickham St George has been the catalyst for me in achieving this amazing goal. Even though Kez lives in Australia, and I live in the United States, together we have made this book become a reality, one of the fantastic things about technology! If you are looking to achieve your goal of authoring a book and especially want to share your story, then Kez Wickham St. George is the one you want as your structural editor / Publisher. She is an absolute joy to work with; I highly recommend Kez!

www.ingramcontent.com/pod-product-compliance
Lightning Source LLC
Chambersburg PA
CBHW060401080526
44583CB00012B/421